Upper Columbia Basin Network
Aspen Monitoring Annual Report 2010

Craters of the Moon National Monument and Preserve (CRMO)

UPPER COLUMBIA
BASIN NETWORK
UCBN

Natural Resource Technical Report NPS/UCBN/NRTR—2011/456

Eva K. Strand, Ph.D.
Wildland Fire Program
University of Idaho
Moscow, Idaho 83844-1135

Stephen C. Bunting, Ph.D
Rangeland Ecology and Management Program
University of Idaho
Moscow, Idaho 83844-1135

Leigh Ann Starcevich, Ph.D.
PO Box 1032
Corvallis, Oregon 97339

June 2011

U.S. Department of the Interior
National Park Service
Natural Resource Program Center
Fort Collins, Colorado

Contents

Figures

Tables

Appendices

Executive Summary

The mission of the National Park Service is "to conserve unimpaired the natural and cultural resources and values of the national park system for the enjoyment of this and future generations" (NPS 1999). To uphold this goal, the Director of the NPS approved the Natural Resource Challenge to encourage national parks to focus on the preservation of the nation's natural heritage through science, natural resource inventories, and expanded resource monitoring (NPS 1999). Through the Challenge, 270 parks in the national park system were organized into 32 inventory and monitoring networks.

The Upper Columbia Basin Network (UCBN) has identified 14 priority vital signs, indicators of ecosystem health, which represent a broad suite of ecological phenomena operating across multiple temporal and spatial scales. Quaking aspen is one particularly high priority vital sign for two UCBN parks, City of Rocks National Reserve (CIRO) and Craters of the Moon National Monument and Preserve (CRMO). Aspen is a focal resource at CIRO and CRMO because of its biological and aesthetic significance. Although aspen comprise only a small percentage of the land cover in the parks, the community type contributes significantly to species diversity and richness. Current observations of aspen decline and die-off in the western states are of concern to natural resource managers and scientists.

The sampling design for aspen is divided into three sampling panels. Panel 1 consists of aspen stands in CRMO while panel 2 and 3 consist of aspen stands in CIRO. In 2007, 108 plots in 22 stands were sampled in CRMO. Panel 2, consisting of 86 plots in 16 stands in CIRO, was sampled in 2008, and panel 3 consisting of 45 plots in 8 stands in CIRO was sampled in 2009. Details regarding the sampling in CIRO in 2008 and 2009 are available in annual reports from previous years (Strand and Bunting 2008; Strand and Bunting 2009). This annual report details the 2010 status estimates in CRMO and a statistical change analysis comparing sampled stands in CRMO in 2007 and 2010. During the field season 2010 we re-sampled 102 plots in 21 stands in CRMO that were previously sampled in 2007. In 2010 we decided to remove CRMO stand #34, located on Big Cinder Butte, from the sampling protocol and future analyses because of the difficult access and unstable soil and cinder substrate on Big Cinder Butte.

The park average stem densities (stems per hectare) for aspen and conifer species for the 2007 and 2010 sampling seasons in CRMO are summarized in the table below.

Park	Species	Year	Suckers[1]	Regeneration[2]	Mature[3]	Dead[4]
CRMO	Aspen	2007	4,839	1,545	818	1,009
CRMO	Aspen	2010	5,412	1,761	698	923
CRMO	Conifer	2007	48	6	14	20
CRMO	Conifer	2010	68	14	8	0

[1] Suckers include suckers or seedlings < 5 feet tall. A sucker is an aspen shoot originating from vegetative sprouting from another aspen tree.
[2] Regeneration includes trees greater than 2.5 cm (1 inch) in diameter breast height (dbh) and shorter than 75% of the stand height.
[3] Mature trees are greater than 2.5 cm (1 inch) in dbh and taller than 75% of the stand height.
[4] Dead stems are greater than 2.5 cm (1 inch) in dbh.

The aspen protocol (Strand et al. 2009) was approved in September 2009. The methods presented in this report reflect that version, version 1.0 of the protocol. The majority of the aspen stands sampled in CRMO in 2010 is regenerating and contain a distribution of age classes. There are however stands with relatively low aspen stem densities, low regeneration, and/or high numbers of dead aspen stems. Stand #13 has no mature stems although suckering (2056 stems/ha) and regeneration (3117 stems/ha) is adequate, indicating that the stand likely will recover. Stand #5 and #26 have low regeneration counts, 647 stems/ha and 282 stems/ha, respectively.

The data from 2007 and 2010 were tested for a change in stem counts of aspen and conifers within size groups, rather than a linear trend because only two years of data are currently available. Zero-inflation models were applied for the conifer analysis because of the large number of plots that contained zero conifer stems. As more monitoring data become available, more complex models may be applied. Plot-level covariates were included in the analysis because they may be useful for modeling the mean structure of aspen stem counts.

For a Type I error of 0.05, no significant change in aspen stem counts was detected across age groups using plot level or stand level means. A significant change in aspen regeneration counts was found for both analyses. A significant change was also detected when analyzing raw counts for both aspen suckers and mature trees, but this result was not obtained for the analysis of stand-level means. No significant change was found for dead aspen trees in either analysis. No significant change in conifer counts across age groups was detected while a significant increase in mature conifers was detected.

Aspen stem counts were correlated with the stand level environmental variables elevation, slope and aspect. For the analysis of the raw plot-level counts, the slope of the site was determined to correlate significantly with regeneration counts, and site elevation correlates with counts of mature trees. Plot-level counts were modeled as functions of fixed-year variables and site-level covariates (slope, elevation, and/or aspect) with the exception of the model for suckers which only includes a fixed-stand effect. Models of stand-level means by age group incorporated stand effects for all age groups except regeneration which only included a fixed-year effect.

Acknowledgements

Funding for this project was provided through the National Park Service Natural Resource Challenge and the Servicewide Inventory and Monitoring Program. We thank the Upper Columbia Basin Network program leader Lisa Garrett for encouragement, provision of resources and fruitful discussions and data manager Gordon Dicus for development and maintenance of the aspen database and invaluable assistance with data quality assurance and control. We thank the staff at Craters of the Moon National Monument and Preserve for contributions and critique of the aspen monitoring protocol and annual reports, and for assistance during field reconnaissance. Thank you to the field assistants and summer interns that worked in CRMO during the summers of 2007 and 2010, you contributed immensely to field data collection, data recording, and fun.

Introduction

Aspen Ecology and Rationale for Monitoring

Quaking aspen (*Populus tremuloides*) is a member of the willow (*Salicaceae*) family and is the most widespread deciduous tree in North America (Little 1971). Although the geographic range is large, aspen's high evapotranspiration demands limit the species to areas where the annual precipitation exceeds 400 mm (DeByle 1985), wet micro sites near streams or springs, and areas where snow melt contributes to water availability throughout the dry months.

The life cycle of quaking aspen in the West is unique. Although aspen is a prolific producer of viable seed, conditions required for successful germination and establishment of aspen are rare in the West (Kemperman and Barnes 1976; Romme 1982; Mitton and Grant 1996). Many botanists argue that significant sexual reproduction in aspen has not occurred in the western United States within the last 10,000 years, since the last glacial retreat (Einspahr and Winton 1976; McDonough 1985). An example of recent successful establishments of aspen seedlings followed the severe fires in Yellowstone in 1988, which apparently provided a 'window of opportunity' of suitable substrate and climate conditions (Romme et al. 2005). The primary means of aspen reproduction in the West is via vegetative root suckering (Bartos 2001). While limited vegetative reproduction occurs within many established stands, prolific vegetative reproduction in aspen clones is thought to require disturbance to promote suckering. Mortality of individual aspen stems caused by disturbance interrupts the balance between the two hormones auxin and cytokinin such that when mature aspen trees are killed or stressed the flow of auxin is suppressed and cytokinin can begin to stimulate root suckering (Bartos 2001). According to Barnes (1975) aspen clones can exist as self-regenerating organisms for thousands of years through periodic disturbance. Although aspen clones are long-lived, individual aspen stems are short-lived, normally living 100-150 years (Shepperd et al. 2001) with some occasionally exceeding 200 years (Mueggler 1989). Since sexual regeneration requires prolonged moist conditions and is extremely rare for intermountain western aspen, an aspen clone lost from the landscape will generally not regenerate from seed (Mitton and Grant 1996).

Aspen stands in the western mountains commonly occur in conjunction with conifer species but have also been observed as uneven-aged aspen stands where aspen appears to persist as a stable, self-regenerating ecosystem (Rogers et al. 2010). These stable aspen systems are unsuitable for conifers or are far away from conifer seed sources (Mueggler 1989). In biophysical settings where aspen is seral to conifer species, slow-growing shade tolerant conifers begin to overtop aspen late in succession and will eventually outcompete and lead to aspen loss (Shepperd et al. 2001). Shepperd et al. (2001) show that aspen growth rates are independent of conifer presence in early to mid-succession and estimate that conifers will begin to out-compete aspen at a stand age of 100-150 years.

Browsing by wildlife and livestock has been shown to inhibit successful regeneration in aspen stands (Bartos and Campbell 1998; Kay and Bartos 2000; Kaye et al. 2005; Jones et al. 2009). Growth in aspen suckers is reduced when browsing results in removal of terminal leaders and large amounts of branch biomass (Jones et al. 2009). Browsing during mid-season over consecutive years and repeated browsing in the same growing season should be avoided in areas where aspen regeneration is a management goal (Jones et al. 2009). Aspen regeneration is particularly affected within elk (*Cervus elaphus*) winter range in areas when elk populations are high and where elk are not hunted (Hart and Hart 2001). Recent research (Kaye et al. 2005) confirms that high levels of elk browsing and conifer dominance negatively influence aspen establishment but do not affect the growth or mortality of individual mature aspen ramets.

Drought within the past decade has been reported to cause mortality in aspen in Colorado (Worrall et al. 2008) and in the Canadian parklands (Brandt et al. 2003; Frey et al. 2004). In Colorado, mature stands on south-facing slopes at low elevation were found to be particularly susceptible to disease and insects as a result of acute drought and high temperatures. Aspen dieback in Canada has been correlated to factors such as stand age, drought and freeze-thaw events, defoliation, wood-boring insects, and fungal pathogens (Brandt et al. 2003; Frey et al. 2004). Rising temperatures and drought have also been correlated with increased forest mortality in the southwestern U.S. (van Mantgem and Stephenson 2007; van Mantgem et. al. 2009).

A recent phenomenon affecting western aspen is referred to as *aspen die-off* and is different from the slow decline in aspen populations that has been occurring over the past century. In cases of *aspen die-off* mature aspen stems are dying with no apparent regeneration in the form of suckering (http://www.fs.fed.us/rmrs/docs/congressional-briefing/issues/aspen-die-off.pdf). Scientists and managers are currently researching the causes, trying to find solutions to this die-off, currently affecting as much as 10% of western aspen stands (http://spectre.nmsu.edu/dept/docs/forest/AspenDieOff.pdf). In the summer of 2010 USFS forest pathologist Jim Worall reported that the spread of the *aspen die-off* appears to have stopped in Colorado; however, damage continues in affected areas (http://www.waterinfo.org/node/4609).

Aspen is an important resource to City of Rocks National Reserve (CIRO) and Craters of the Moon National Monument and Preserve (CRMO) because of its biological and aesthetic significance. Although aspen comprise only a small percentage of the land cover in the parks, the community type contributes significantly to species diversity and richness (Shive and Peterson 2001; Madison et al. 2003). Aspen brings visitors to the western mountains and parks, improves local economies, inspires poets and artists, and is portrayed in modern stories as well as tribal myths (McCool 2001). Aspen is an important attraction for campers, naturalists, and recreationists in the otherwise semi-arid landscapes of CIRO and CRMO.

The Upper Columbia Basin Network (UCBN) has identified 14 priority vital signs to monitor (Garret et al. 2007). Aspen exhibits a relatively slow range of change compared to other vital signs and covers a greater spatial extent in the two parks where it is monitored. Information gained from monitoring aspen will contribute to the weight of ecological knowledge about natural resources at CIRO and CRMO and to regional management strategies for the conservation of aspen. In particular, aspen in CIRO and CRMO occur in areas that are near or below the precipitation threshold of 400 mm per year (Perala 1990) where upland aspen can persist long-term. A warming climate may result in a reduced snow pack, which could affect the availability of water for aspen stands in the parks. Aspen in these parks may be one of the first species to respond to locally changing climate, and the response may be a decline in regeneration or a die-off of water stressed clones. It is not currently known how aspen will react to a changing climate, and the trends observed, as part of this monitoring protocol, may contribute valuable data to future aspen management in the western United States.

Objectives

The overarching programmatic goal of the UCBN aspen vital signs monitoring program is to obtain data that will inform management decisions pertaining to the perpetuation of quaking aspen populations at CIRO and CRMO. The aspen protocol (Strand et al. 2009) was approved in September 2009 and the methods presented in this report reflect that version, version 1.0 of the protocol. The monitoring protocol addresses the following specific measurable monitoring objectives:

- Estimate current status and long-term trend in regeneration of park aspen populations as well as individual stands.
- Estimate status and trend in aspen abundance, as measured by stem density of live and dead trees, within aspen stands. Specifically, live aspen stems will be counted in five size classes: Class I - suckers or seedlings < 46 cm (1.5 ft) tall, Class II - suckers or seedlings 46 - 152 cm (1.5-5 ft) tall, Class III - greater than 152 cm (5 ft) and up to 2.5 cm (1 inch) in diameter at breast height (dbh), Class IV - greater than 152 cm (5 ft) and > 2.5 cm (1 inch) in diameter at breast height (dbh) but < 75% of the stand height, Class V - greater than 2.5 cm (1 inch) in dbh and > 75% of the stand height.
- Estimate the status and trend in dead standing aspen stems.
- Estimate the status and trend of conifer density within aspen stands.

The following statistical sampling objectives have been developed for this protocol:

- Estimate with 90% confidence the mean, $\hat{\mu}$, within $\pm$ 25% of the true mean, μ, for aspen stem density (stems/ha) of suckers (Class I+II), regeneration (Class III+IV), mature trees (Class V) and dead stems within aspen clones.
- Detect with >80% certainty (power, or 1-β) a change $\geq$ 25% between any two sequential time periods (5 years) of mean aspen live or dead stem density estimates with a 0.10 acceptable false-change (α) error rate. All upland aspen stands, larger than 0.3 ha in size, that are not located in entirely in riparian areas or composed of shrubby snow-damaged aspen will be sampled. The difficult access and ecologically sensitive location on Big Cinder Butte in CRMO prevents us from including this stand in the sampling frame.

Methods

Field data collection

Sampling methods followed those detailed by Strand et al. (2009). All aspen stands available for sampling were classified via remote sensing, delineated on aerial photos or via a Global Positioning System unit (GPS) in the field in the CRMO (Figure 1) in 2006. According to the protocol revisit design (Table 1) panel 1 in CRMO was sampled in 2007, and panel 2 and 3 were sampled in CIRO in 2008 and 2009. During the field season 2010, the stands in CRMO were re-visited for the first time, three years after permanent markers were established in 2007. Once baseline data has been collected over two time periods (2007-2009) and (2010-2012) for each stand, sampling will continue on a 5-year cycle.

Table 1. Proposed revisit design for CRMO and CIRO. The first two sampling sessions will follow a [1-2] revisit design. Subsequent sampling sessions will follow a [1-4] revisit design in which one panel is located in CRMO and two panels are located in CIRO.

| | Sampling Occasion (Year) | | | | | | | | | | |
Panel	2007	2008	2009	2010	2011	2012	2013	2014	2015	2016	2017
1 - CRMO	X			X					X		
2 - CIRO1		X			X					X	
3 - CIRO2			X			X					X

Permanent sampling transects were established within aspen stands in CIRO and CRMO in 2007-2009. The number of transects established in each stand was determined by completing a power analysis that allowed for detection of trend with statistical confidence (0.90) and power (0.80) while minimizing the sampling effort. The number of transects placed in each stand was further weighted by the area of the stand such that more transects were placed in larger stands. The starting point for each transect was randomly located within the stand boundary and transects were oriented north-south or east-west depending on the orientation of the stand. Four plots were placed along each transect with a distance of 25 m between plot centers. Based on a variogram analysis, plots located at least 25 m apart can be considered spatially independent (Strand et al. 2009). The number of transects within each aspen stand was determined via the power analysis and then weighted by the areal extent of the stand. Altogether 108 plots were placed within 22 stands in CRMO in 2007 (Figure 1) and in 2010, 102 of those plots were re-visited (Figure 2-4). Stand #34 located on Big Cinder Butte was not re-sampled in 2010 due to difficult access and unstable substrate composed of cinder.

The numbers of aspen and conifer stems within pre-determined size classes (Table 2) that were rooted or had at least 50% of the stem diameter at ground level rooted within the 4-m radius plot were counted. Conifer plants shorter than 15 cm above ground were not counted. Dead stems that were lying on the ground were not counted; however, dead stems that were leaning or otherwise partially standing were counted, if they were rooted or had at least 50% of the stem diameter at ground level rooted in the plot.

It should be noted that in 2007 in CRMO, permanent markers were only established for the first plot in each transect. Due to difficulties in relocating plots, additional plots were monumented in

2008. As a consequence, measurements in plots numbered 2, 3, or 4 in each transect, may not have been taken exactly at the same location in 2010 as in 2007.

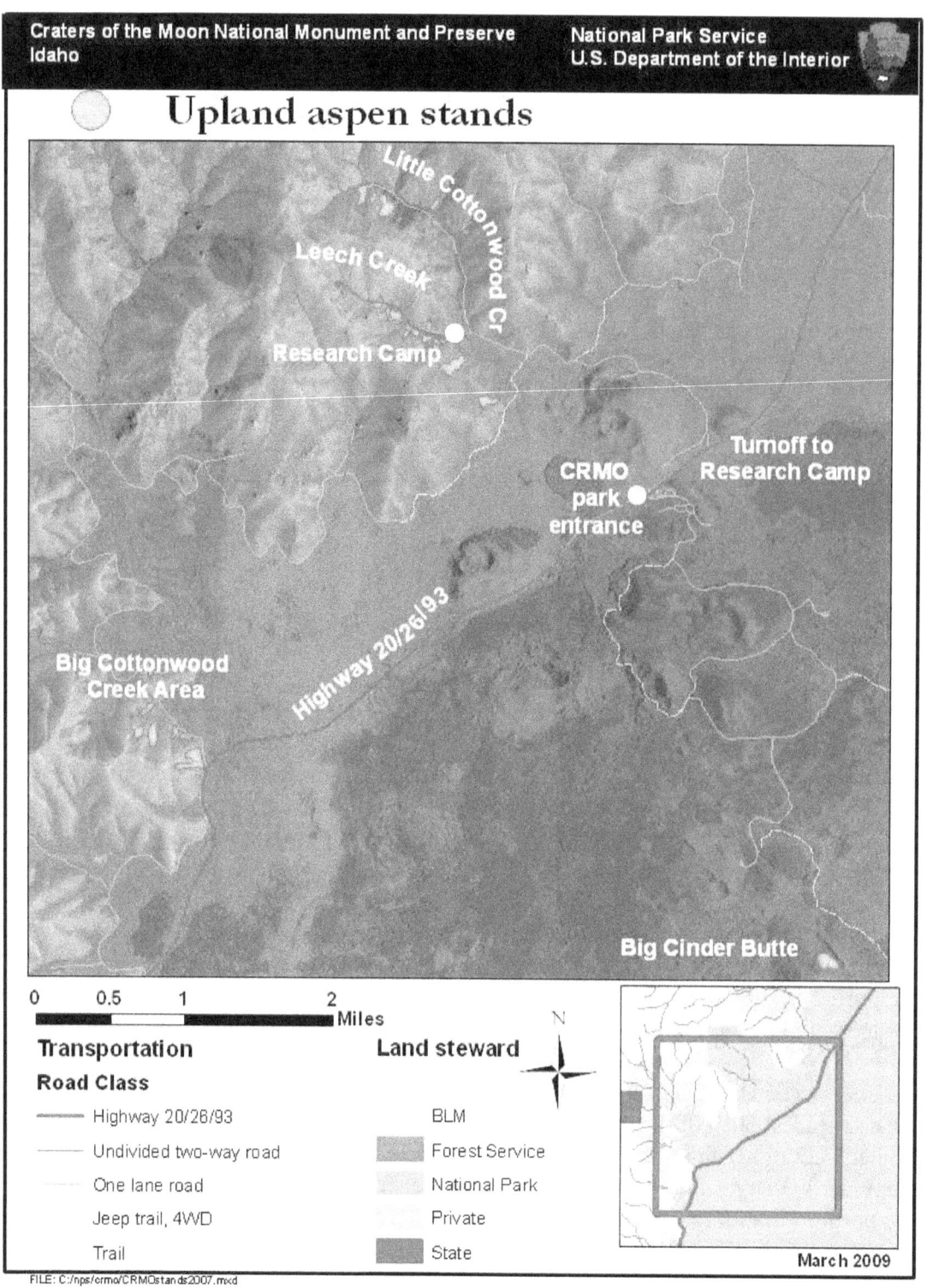

Figure 1. Map of aspen stands in CRMO. Stands are located in the Leech Creek, Little Cottonwood Creek, and Big Cottonwood Creek drainages. The aspen stand on Big Cinder Butte was removed from the CRMO sampling panel in 2010.

Table 2. Size classes of aspen and conifer stems.

Class I	Suckers or seedlings < 46 cm (1.5 ft) tall. Conifer seedlings shorter than 15 cm (6 inches) are not counted due to uncertainty in survival
Class II	Suckers or seedlings < 46 - 152 cm (1.5-5 ft) tall
Class III	Greater than 152 cm (5 ft) and up to 2.5 cm (1 inch) in dbh (diameter at breast height)
Class IV	Greater than 2.5 cm (1 inch) in dbh and shorter than 75% of the stand height
Class V	Greater than 2.5 cm (1 inch) in dbh and taller than 75% of the stand height
Class VI	Dead stems > 2.5 cm (1 inch) in dbh

Aspen total stem density by size class was calculated for each transect, for each stand, and for the entire park, by adding all individual aspen stems within the sampled area and then dividing by the total sampled area (sum of sampled area within transect, stand, or park). Summary statistics are reported for four combinations of size classes as follows: Suckers (Class I+II), Regeneration (Class III+IV), Mature trees (Class V) and Dead stems (Class VI).

A distance photo of each aspen stand was taken from a location with a good vantage point that overlooked the stand. The UTM coordinates, NAD83 datum, and true north azimuth in the direction the photo was oriented are recorded. The locations for the distance photos are mapped in Figure 2-4.

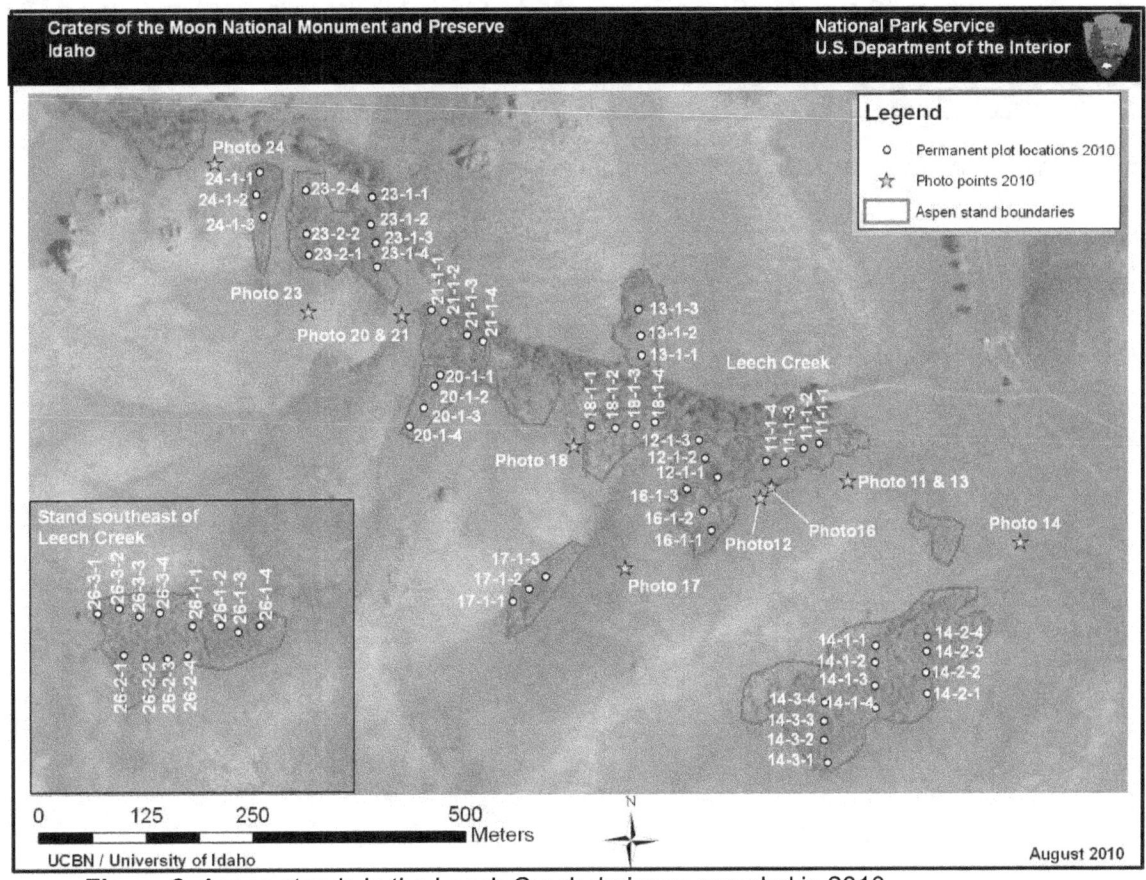

Figure 2. Aspen stands in the Leech Creek drainage sampled in 2010.

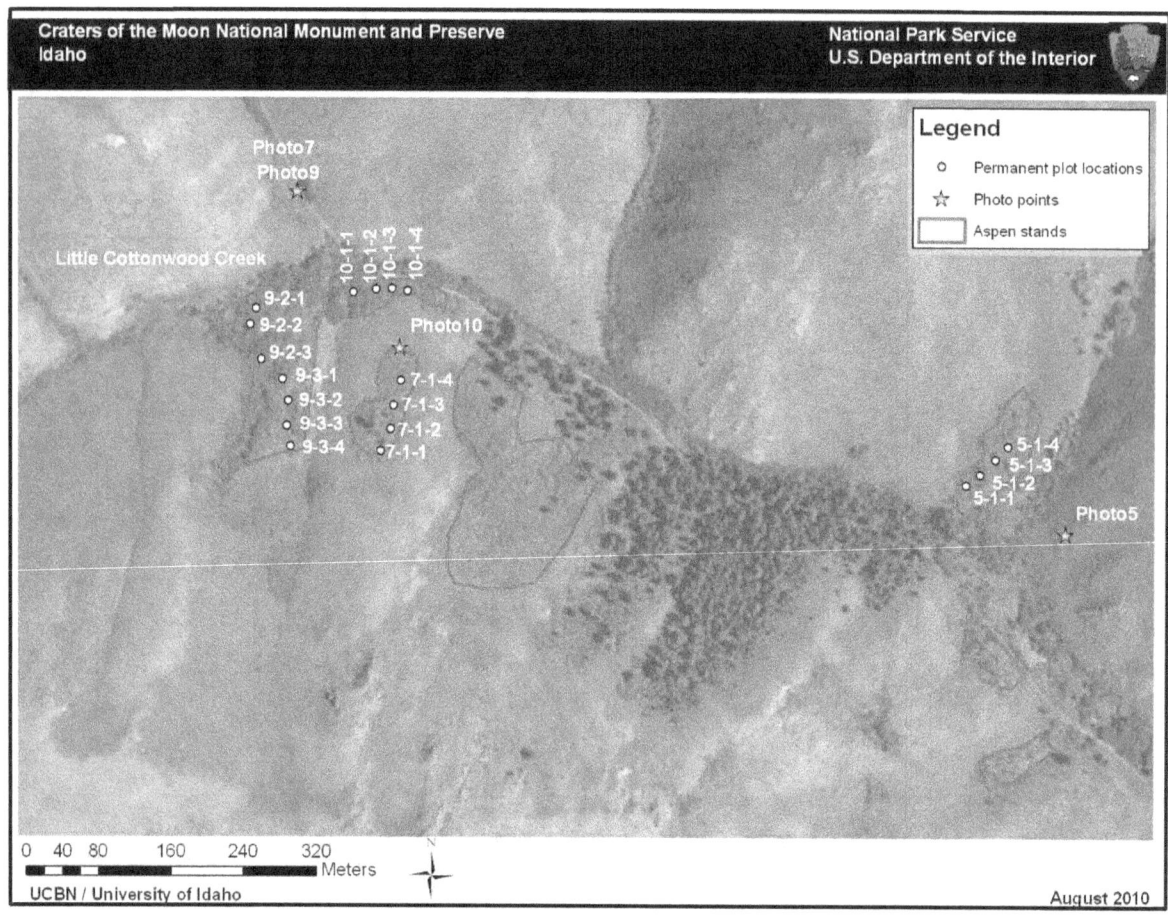

Figure 3. Aspen stands in the Little Cottonwood drainage sampled in 2010.

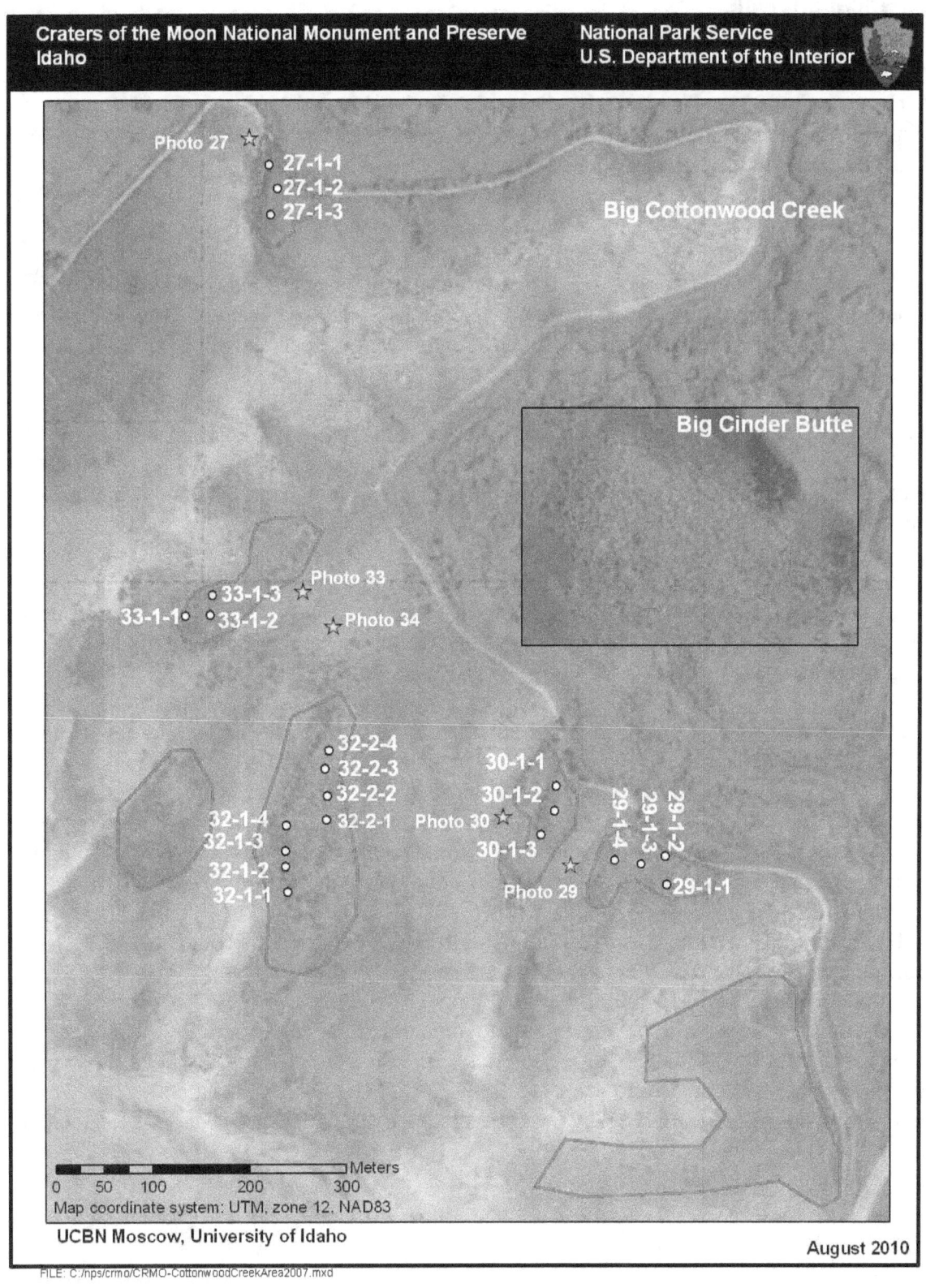

Figure 4. Aspen stands in the Cottonwood drainage sampled in 2010.

Statistical analysis

UCBN personnel plan to monitor trends in counts of aspen and conifer tree stems in CRMO and CIRO. A total of 22 stands larger than 0.3 ha in size has been identified in CRMO; these stands did not include aspen stands on private land, in riparian areas, stands smaller than 0.3 ha, or those damaged by snow. Transects in 21 of these 22 stands were visited in both 2007 and 2010. Data from these 21 aspen stands were used to test for a change between the two years. When more years of monitoring data are available, then tests for linear trends in time will be conducted.

The response design incorporates one to three transects per aspen stand with the number of transects chosen proportionally to the size of each stand. Four to twelve plots were located within each stand. The outcome of interest is the number of aspen and conifer stems, and these counts are obtained within each plot (Figure 5).

Covariates include stand elevation, slope, aspect, and height. These covariates were collected at the stand level and do not vary within a stand or across years. The aspen height covariate is not complete for all stands so it is not used to avoid the omission of stand counts during data analysis.

Stem counts for 2007 and 2010 were compared for four age groups: suckers, regeneration, mature trees, and dead trees (Figure 6). The year effect is examined across all age groups using age group as a model covariate and independently within each age group. Inference on the change between years is also desired across stands and within each stand.

The aspen stem data were analyzed in two different ways: raw counts at the plot level and stand-level means calculated for each age classification. Because 16 of the 21 stands include only a single transect, comparisons among transects within a stand was not possible. Therefore, no transect effect may be modeled for the stand-level stem counts. A test of the null hypothesis of no difference in aspen stem counts versus the two-sided alternative hypothesis of a difference in either direction is conducted to assess change in stem counts between 2007 and 2010.

Model selection from a range of fixed and random effects models was conducted using Bayes Information Criterion (BIC) (Gurka, 2006). For models with similar BIC values, R^2 values for each model were also considered. If the final model selected with BIC did not contain a term for the year, then the final model was compared to an identical model, except for the inclusion of the fixed year effect. If the final model selected with BIC did contain one or more terms for year, then that model was compared to the same model less the terms associated with year. The models were compared using an F-test which tests the overall effect of year between the two years rather than a linear trend.

Figure 5. Plot-level counts of aspen trees for 2007 and 2010

Figure 6. Histograms of differences in mean aspen counts by age group (2010 mean aspen count – 2007 mean aspen count)

Conifer counts for 2007 and 2010 were also compared for four age groups: suckers, regeneration, mature trees, and dead trees. The year effect was examined across all age groups using age group as a model covariate and independently within each age group. Inference on the change between years was also desired across stands and within each stand.

Model selection began with a simple linear regression of the stand-level mean count on the year indicator and age group factor. Skewness was addressed by using the transformation $\log(Y + 1)$ for stand-level means. Since the means are real-valued, a zero-inflated lognormal distribution was also fit to the stand-level means. The large proportion of zeros in the stand-level conifer count means (Table 3) were evident in residual plots from simple linear regression models, indicating that model assumptions for transformed and untransformed were not met. Several zero-inflated lognormal models were considered with indicators for year and age group used as predictors in the models for zero inflation and the lognormal outcome in the analysis of stand-level means across age groups. The final model for the analysis across age groups included an indicator for the sucker age group in the zero-inflation model and an indicator for the year in the lognormal model. Within each age group analysis, the year indicator was used for the lognormal model and the proportion of zeros was estimated as a constant across sites. When more years are data are available, more complex models for the zero inflation and the lognormal random variable may be considered and trend in the presence of conifers may also be estimated and tested. The likelihood ratio test was used to assess the significance of the year term in the model for mean conifer counts at the stand level.

Table 3. Proportion of zeros for stand-level conifer tree count means

Age Group	2007	2010
Suckers	0.67	0.57
Regeneration	0.95	0.86
Mature	0.95	0.86
Dead	0.90	1.00
All	0.87	0.82

Results

Park and stand level stem counts

During the 2010 field season, 102 plots in 21 stands in CRMO were re-visited. These plots were permanently marked and established in 2007. See Appendix A for a summary of all mapped aspen stands in CRMO, whether they are sampled or not and reasons for not sampling.

Aspen total stem density by size class was calculated for each stand by adding all individual aspen stems within the sampled area and then dividing by the total sampled area (sum of sampled area within stand). Summary statistics are reported in stems/ha for four combinations of size classes as follows: Suckers (Class I+II), Regeneration (Class III+IV), Mature trees (Class V) and Dead stems (Class VI) for CRMO during the sampling seasons 2007 and 2010 (Table 4) and by stand (Table 5 and 6). The difference in aspen stem density between 2007 and 2010 is listed in Table 7.

Table 4. Park stem count averages for the 2007 and 2010 sampling effort for aspen and conifer species.

Park	Species	Year	Suckers[1]	Regeneration[2]	Mature[3]	Dead[4]
CRMO	Aspen	2007	4,839	1,545	818	1,009
CRMO	Aspen	2010	5,412	1,761	698	923
CRMO	Conifer	2007	48	6	14	20
CRMO	Conifer	2010	68	14	8	0

[1] Suckers include suckers or seedlings < 5 feet tall. A sucker is an aspen shoot originating from vegetative sprouting from another aspen tree.
[2] Regeneration includes trees greater than 2.5 cm (1 inch) in diameter breast height (dbh) and shorter than 75% of the stand height.
[3] Mature trees are greater than 2.5 cm (1 inch) in dbh and taller than 75% of the stand height.
[4] Dead stems are greater than 2.5 cm (1 inch) in dbh.

In 2010, the lowest regeneration was observed in stand #5 (647 stems/ha) and #26 (282 stems/ha), stand #26 also showed the lowest suckering level (846 stems/ha). The lowest count of mature stems was recorded in stand #5 (99 stems/ha) and stand #13 (0 stems/ha).

Conifers were present at low densities in 13 of the 21 sampled stands in CRMO in 2010 (Table 6). Rocky mountain juniper (*Juniperus scopulorum*) was present in two stands (# 26 and 32), limber pine (*Pinus flexilis*) was present in nine stands (#10, 11,12,14,16, 20, 26, 27, and 30) and Douglas-fir (*Pseudotsuga menziesii*) was present in two stands (#7 and 10). Three stands contained mature conifer stems (#11, 26, and 30).

Paired photographs of the aspen stands sampled in 2007 and 2010 are compiled in Appendix B.

Table 5. Aspen stem density in stems per hectare in CRMO stands sampled in 2007 and 2010.

Stand	Suckers 2007	Regen. 2007	Mature 2007	Dead 2007	Suckers 2010	Regen. 2010	Mature 2010	Dead 2010
5	2188	348	348	249	3780	647	99	398
7	7361	2636	398	2636	2934	4128	298	945
9	4775	1393	895	1061	3808	2529	824	1847
10	4974	2387	1492	1790	2039	3084	945	1840
11	9276	920	1219	1343	14821	995	1542	647
12	3846	398	663	862	4178	1658	663	398
13	3050	796	0	133	2056	3117	0	0
14	3888	597	669	723	8140	1127	713	448
16	7759	796	464	133	6565	2586	332	265
17	3647	66	1127	2188	7361	928	398	1857
18	5322	2537	249	448	4526	3929	348	348
20	14622	2835	547	1243	19894	4128	249	1094
21	1492	3034	796	50	4377	2288	149	647
23	1865	2014	1293	746	3098	1279	654	881
24	1393	729	862	995	995	1194	796	663
26	497	431	1459	1111	846	282	1376	1144
27	2719	1459	1393	1326	1459	995	1658	597
29	13180	995	547	1592	11937	2039	696	2089
30	2387	1790	928	531	4775	1724	862	1393
32	6913	1542	448	1194	7063	1815	547	1044
33	11870	8555	862	1393	10544	11539	1459	2653

Table 6. Conifer stem density in stems per hectare in CRMO stands sampled in 2007 and 2010.

Stand	Suckers 2007	Regen. 2007	Mature 2007	Dead 2007	Suckers 2010	Regen. 2010	Mature 2010	Dead 2010
5	0	0	0	0	149	0	0	0
7	0	0	0	0	149	0	0	0
9	0	0	232	0	149	0	0	0
10	0	0	0	0	149	99	0	0
11	50	0	0	0	0	50	50	0
12	133	0	0	0	133	0	0	0
13	0	0	0	0	0	0	0	0
14	90	0	0	0	182	66	0	0
16	0	0	0	0	265	0	0	0
17	0	0	0	0	0	0	0	0
18	0	0	0	0	0	0	0	0
20	50	0	0	0	50	0	0	0
21	0	0	0	0	0	0	0	0
23	0	0	0	0	0	0	0	0
24	0	0	0	199	0	0	0	0
26	149	50	0	0	99	0	33	0
27	199	0	0	0	265	0	0	0
29	0	0	0	0	0	0	0	0
30	0	0	0	0	0	0	66	0
32	75	0	0	0	25	0	0	0
33	0	0	0	464	0	0	0	0

Table 7. Difference in stem density (stems/ha) in CRMO between 2007 and 2010. Positive numbers means an increase in stem density from 2007 to 2010.

Stand	Suckers 2010-2007	Regeneration 2010-2007	Mature 2010-2007	Dead 2010-2007
5	1592	298	-249	149
7	-4427	1492	-99	-1691
9	-966	1137	-71	786
10	-2934	696	-547	50
11	5546	75	323	-696
12	332	1260	0	-464
13	-995	2321	0	-133
14	4252	531	44	-276
16	-1194	1791	-133	133
17	3714	862	-729	-332
18	-796	1393	99	-99
20	5272	1293	-298	-149
21	2885	-746	-647	597
23	1233	-735	-639	135
24	-398	464	-66	-332
26	348	-149	-83	33
27	-1260	-464	265	-729
29	-1243	1044	149	497
30	2387	-66	-66	862
32	149	274	99	-149
33	-1326	2984	597	1260

Statistical analysis of change, 2007 to 2010

The effect of stands was treated as fixed since the population of interest was nearly censused and therefore the sample is not representative of a larger population of aspen stands. Residual diagnostics indicated that a logarithmic transformation of raw plot-level counts and stand-level means better met assumptions for multiple linear regression models. Repeated measures analysis of raw plot-level data indicated no significant correlation among plot measurements within a stand when the compound symmetric correlation structure was considered. More complex spatial correlation structures cannot be assessed without location data. Because potential predictors were measured at the stand level and do not vary over time, regression models of stand means by year may either include the fixed stand effect or the stand-level covariates but not both.

Change in time across aspen age groups

For the analysis of the raw plot-level aspen stem counts, the model selected from comparisons of BIC included fixed effects for each age group and for each stand. The test of change between 2007 and 2010 for log transformed stem counts was inconclusive for detecting a difference in stem counts between the two years ($F = 3.3421$, $df = 1$ and 958, p-value $= 0.0678$). The analysis of stand-level means across groups was conducted with a model including only fixed effects for each age group. The F-test for change between 2007 and 2010 indicated no significant change at the alpha $= 0.05$ level ($F = 0.8202$, $df = 1$ and 160, p-value $= 0.3665$).

Change in time within aspen age groups

Data from each age group were analyzed independently to determine if changes in aspen stem counts occurred between 2007 and 2010. When raw plot-level counts were examined for suckers, a significant year effect was found when comparing models with fixed effects for each stand ($F = 4.9034$, $df = 1$ and 335, p-value $= 0.0275$). The final model for regeneration included a fixed effect of year and an effect for the slope of the site. The slope effect was negative, indicating that steeper slopes are predictors of lower aspen stem counts (slope coefficient $= -0.0295$, SE $= 0.0091$). The test for differences between 2007 and 2010 regeneration counts were significant at the 0.05 level ($F = 4.1919$, $df = 1$ and 275, p-value $= 0.0416$). The model for plot-level counts of mature aspen trees included the year effect and a fixed coefficient for elevation. This coefficient was negative, indicating decreasing mature tree counts with increasing elevation (elevation coefficient $= -0.0018$, SE $= 0.0007$). The test for differences between 2007 and 2010 mature tree counts was significant at the 0.05 level ($F = 6.6693$, $df = 2$ and 166, p-value $= 0.0016$). The final model for dead trees counted at the plot level included fixed effects for year, elevation, slope, and aspect but the test of the year effect was not significant at the 0.05 level ($F = 0.0393$, $df = 1$ and 174, p-value $= 0.8430$).

When stand-level means were analyzed, the evidence was less convincing for between-year differences within age groups. The final model for suckers included fixed effects for year and stand, but the F-test obtained from comparing the final model with the model excluding the fixed year effect was not significant at the 0.05 level ($F = 1.3179$, $df = 1$ and 20, p-value $= 0.2645$). For regeneration, stand-level means were modeled only as a function of the year effect.

Comparison with model including only an overall mean provided evidence of a difference between the two years ($F = 5.0878$, $df = 1$ and 40, p-value = 0.0296). The analysis of stand-level means of mature tree counts, modeled as a function of fixed year and stand effects, did not provide overwhelming evidence of a difference between years ($F = 4.0132$, $df = 1$ and 19, p-value = 0.0596). Stand-level means of dead tree counts were modeled only as a function of fixed stands effects and did not exhibit evidence of a change between 2007 and 2010 ($F = 0.1623$, $df = 1$ and 19, p-value = 0.6916).

Change in time by aspen stand and age group

Testing changes in aspen counts was also of interest for each aspen stand. The need for a separate slope for each stand was assessed by testing if the fixed year-stand interaction was significantly different than 0. There was little evidence to suggest that changes occurred between years for the analysis of plot-level aspen counts ($F = 0.4947$, $df = 20$ and 941, p-value = 0.9693) and the analysis of stand-level means ($F = 0.2499$, $df = 20$ and 123, p-value = 0.9996). Examining the raw plot-level counts within each age group, no evidence was found to suggest that slopes should be modeled individually for each stand for suckers ($F = 1.3946$, $df = 20$ and 315, p-value = 0.1223), regeneration ($F = 0.5493$, $df = 20$ and 236, p-value = 0.9424), mature trees ($F = 0.6267$, $df = 19$ and 129, p-value = 0.8802), or dead trees ($F = 1.0578$, $df = 19$ and 138, p-value = 0.4011). Therefore, the fixed year effect across stands may be assumed to apply within stands also.

Change in conifer counts from 2007 to 2010

The likelihood ratio test was used to assess the significance of the year term in the model for mean conifer counts at the stand level (Table 8). The results indicate no significant change in stand-level means of conifer counts between 2007 and 2010 across age groups and within the sucker and regeneration age groups for a Type I error rate of 0.05. However, a significant change was detected for mature conifers with a p-value of 0.0033 for the two-sided test of no change versus a change in either direction. Because no non-zero conifer counts were obtained for dead trees in 2010, the full model with a year term for the lognormal model could not be fit and a test of change between the two years cannot be obtained for dead conifer trees.

Table 8. Results for likelihood ratio tests of change in stand-level conifer means, 2007 and 2010

Age Group	Log-likelihood (full model)	Log-likelihood (reduced model)	Likelihood ratio statistic	p-value
Suckers	-22.5340	-22.7853	0.5027	0.4783
Regeneration	-10.2975	- 10.3229	0.0509	0.8216
Mature	- 9.1561	- 13.4866	8.6610	0.0033
Dead	- 10.0081	- 10.0081	0	NA
All	-62.7136	-63.4028	1.3784	0.2404

Code for the statistical analysis in program R for the aspen stems is available in Appendix C. R code for the zero-inflated lognormal models and the likelihood ratio tests are provided in Appendix D. Note that these functions are specific to the models outlined in this report and apply for data sets with only two years of data. These functions must be amended if more years of data are available, additional covariates are used, or if different models are considered.

Discussion

Future statistical analysis

Overall, the park average for aspen stem densities of suckers and regeneration have increased from 2007 to 2010 and stem densities for mature and dead aspen stems have decreased. The data from 2007 and 2010 were tested for a change rather than a linear trend because only two years of data are currently available. As more monitoring data become available, more complex models may be applied.

In the future we plan to incorporate local climate data as a covariate for trend analysis. Annual climate data from the nearby weather station at CRMO will be included as model covariates. This weather data can be accessed via the online NOAA Climate Reference Network site (http://www.ncdc.noaa.gov/crn/station.htm?stationId=1021), which provides daily temperatures and precipitation information. Plot-level covariates such as dominant understory species may be useful for modeling the mean structure of aspen and conifer stem counts.

Stands of potential concern in CRMO

Although thresholds indicating when management action may be desirable for long-term maintenance of aspen stands at CIRO and CRMO have not been established, the following is a short summary describing stands with the lowest aspen stem densities and low suckering and regeneration for stands sampled in CRMO in 2007 and 2010. Photos of the stands can be found in Appendix B.

Stand #5: The suckering (3780 stems/ha) is slightly below park average but the regeneration (647 stems/ha) was low in this stand. The mature stems density (99 stems/ha) was much below park average (698 stems/ha). The suckering and regeneration have increased from 2007 to 2010, however, the mature stem count has decreased and the dead stem density has increased.

Stand #13: The suckering (2056 stems/ha) and regeneration (3117 stems/ha) do not appear to be a cause of concern. The mature stems density (0 stems/ha) was, however, noteworthy. The sucker density has decreased from 2007 to 2010; however, the regeneration has increased by 2321 stems/ha which may indicate that the stand will recover given time.

Stand #26: The suckering (846 stems/ha) and regeneration (282 stems/ha) was low in this stand. The mature stems density (1376 stems/ha) was, however, above park average (698 stems/ha). The sucker density has increased by 348 stems/ha and the regeneration density has decreased by 149 stems/ha from 2007 to 2010. The mature stem density has decreased by 83 stems/ha. Overall, it appears that the stem counts are on a downward trend in this stand with low recruitment. Wildlife use is apparent in the stand supported by observations of bedding sites, browsing, and scat from elk and deer.

Literature Cited

Barnes, B.V. 1975. Phenotypic variation of trembling aspen in Western North America. Forest Science 22:319-328.

Bartos, D.L. 2001. Landscape Dynamics of Aspen and Conifer Forests. p. 5-14. Sustaining Aspen in Western Landscapes: Symposium Proceedings; 13-15 June 2000; Grand Junction, CO. USDA Forest Service Proceedings RMRS-P-18.

Bartos, D.L., and R.B. Campbell. 1998. Decline of Quaking Aspen in the Interior West – Examples from Utah. Rangelands 20(1): 17-14.

Brandt, J.P., H.F. Cerzke, K.L. Mallett, W.J.A. Volney, and J.D. Weber. 2003. Factors affecting trembling aspen (*Populus tremuloides* Michx.) health in the boreal forest of Alberta, Saskatchewan, and Manitoba, Canada., Forest Ecology and Management 178:287-300.

DeByle N.V. 1985. Water and Watershed. p. 153-160, *in* DeByle and Winokur (Editors) Aspen: Ecology and Management in the Western United States. USDA Forest Service General Technical Report RM-119.

Einspahr D.W., L.L. Winton. 1976. Genetics of quaking aspen. USDA Forest Service Research Paper WO-25. Washington (DC): USDA.

Frey, B.R., V.J. Lieffers, E.H. Hogg, and S.M. Landhäusser. 2004. Predicting landscape patterns of aspen dieback: mechanisms and knowledge gaps. Canadian Journal of Forest Research 34: 1379–1390.

Hart, J.H., and D.L. Hart. 2001. Interaction among cervids, fungi, and aspen in northwest Wyoming, p.197-205, Sustaining Aspen in Western Landscapes: Symposium Proceedings; 13-15 June 2000; Grand Junction, CO. USDA Forest Service Proceedings RMRS-P-18.

Jones B.E., D.F. Lile, and K.W. Tate. 2009. Effects of simulated browsing on aspen regeneration: Implications for restoration. Rangeland Ecology and Management 62:557-563.

Kay, C.E. and D.L. Bartos. 2000. Ungulate herbivory on Utah aspen: Assessment of long term exclosures. Journal of Range Management 53:145-153.

Kaye, M.W., D. Binkley, and T.J. Stohlgren. 2005. Effects of conifers and elk browsing on quaking aspen forests in the central Rocky Mountains, USA. Ecological Applications 15:1284-1295.

Kemperman J.A., and B.V. Barnes. 1976. Clone size in American aspens. Canadian Journal of Botany 54:2603-2607.

Little, E.L., Jr. 1971. Atlas of United States trees: Vol. 1. Conifers and important hardwoods. U.S. Department of Agriculture, Forest Service, Miscellaneous Publications 1146, 9 p. 202 maps. Washington DC. http://climchange.cr.usgs.gov/data/atlas/little/.Accessed 2004 April 19.

Madison, E., K. Oelrich, T. Rodhouse, and L. Garrett. 2003. Mammal Inventories, City of Rocks National Reserve. University of Idaho, Moscow, Idaho. 43 p.

McCool, S.F. 2001. Quaking aspen and the human experience: dimensions, issues, and challenges. Sustaining Aspen in Western Landscapes: Symposium Proceedings.. USDA Forest Service Proceedings RMRS-P-18, Grand Junction, CO, June 13-15, 2000: 147-160.

McDonough W.T. 1985. Sexual reproduction, seeds and seedlings. In N.V. DeByle and R.P. Winokus R.P., editors. Aspen: ecology and management in the western United States. USDA Forest Service General Technical Report RM- 119.

Miller, R.F., J.D. Bates, T.J. Svejcar, F.B. Pierson, and L.E. Eddleman. 2005. Biology, ecology and management of western juniper. Technical Bulletin 152, Oregon State University Agricultural Experiment Station, Corvallis, OR.

Mitton, B.J., and M.C. Grant. 1996. Genetic variation and the natural history of quaking aspen. BioScience 46:25-31.

Mueggler, W.F. 1989. Age distribution and reproduction of intermountain aspen stands. Western Journal of Applied Forestry 4:41-45.

Rogers P.C., A.J. Leffler, and R.J. Ryel. 2010. Landscape assessment of a stable aspen community in southern Utah, USA. Forest Ecology and Management 259:487-495.

Romme W.H. 1982. Fire and landscape diversity in subalpine forests of Yellowstone National Park. Ecological Monographs 52: 199-221.

Romme W.H., M.G. Turner, G.A. Tuskan, and R.A. Reed. 2005. Establishment, persistence, and growth of aspen (*Populus tremuloides*) seedlings in Yellowstone National Park. Ecology, 86:404-418.

Shepperd, W.D., D.L. Bartos, and S.A. Mata. 2001. Above-and below-ground effects of aspen clonal regeneration and succession to conifers. Canadian Journal of Forest Research, 31:739-745.

Shive, J. and C. Peterson. 2001. Herpetological Inventory of the City of Rocks National Reserve. Idaho State University, Pocatello, ID. 64 p.

Strand, E. K., and S. C. Bunting. 2009. Monitoring aspen in the Upper Columbia Basin Network: 2008 monitoring report for City of Rocks National Reserve and Craters of the

Moon National Monument and Preserve. Natural Resource Technical Report NPS/UCBN/NRTR—2009/196. National Park Service, Fort Collins, CO.

Strand, E. K., S. C. Bunting, R. K. Steinhorst, L. K. Garrett, and G. H. Dicus. 2009. Upper Columbia Basin Network aspen monitoring protocol: Narrative version 1.0. Natural Resource Report NPS/UCBN/NRR—2009/147. National Park Service, Fort Collins, CO.

van Mantgem, P. J., and N.L. Stephenson, 2007. Apparent climatically-induced increase of mortality rates in a temperate forest. Ecology Letters 10: 909–916.

van Mantgem, P.J., N.L. Stephenson, J.C. Byrne, L.D., Daniels, J.F. Franklin, P.Z. Fulé, M.E. Harmon, A.J. Larson, J.M. Smith, A.H. Taylor, and T.T. Veblen. 2009. Widespread increase of tree mortality rates in the western United States. Science 323: 521-524.

Worrall, J.J., L. Egeland, T. Eager, R.A. Mask, E.W. Johnson, P.A. Kemp, and W.D. Shepperd. 2008. Rapid mortality of *Populus tremuloides* in southwestern Colorado, USA. Forest Ecology and Management 255:686-696.

Appendix A. Aspen stands in CRMO
(Including explanations of why some stands were not sampled)

Stand #	Area (ha)	Location	Sample	Transects	Plots	Why Not Sample
1	0.35	Little Cottonwood Creek	No	0	0	Riparian
2	0.55	Little Cottonwood Creek	No	0	0	Riparian
3	0.27	Little Cottonwood Creek	No	0	0	Riparian
4	0.24	Little Cottonwood Creek	No	0	0	Shrubby snow damaged aspen
5	0.63	Little Cottonwood Creek	Yes	1	4	
6	0.27	Little Cottonwood Creek	No	0	0	Smaller than 0.3 ha
7	0.48	Little Cottonwood Creek	Yes	1	4	
8	2.41	Little Cottonwood Creek	No	0	0	Shrubby snow damaged aspen
9	1.56	Little Cottonwood Creek	Yes	2	7	
10	0.36	Little Cottonwood Creek	Yes	1	4	
11	0.63	Leech Creek	Yes	1	4	
12	0.41	Leech Creek	Yes	1	3	
13	0.49	Leech Creek	Yes	1	4	
14	2.95	Leech Creek	Yes	3	12	
15	0.20	Leech Creek	No	0	0	Smaller than 0.3 ha
16	0.37	Leech Creek	Yes	1	3	
17	0.39	Leech Creek	Yes	1	3	
18	0.55	Leech Creek	Yes	1	4	
19	0.53	Leech Creek	No	0	4	Riparian
20	0.32	Leech Creek	Yes	1	4	
21	0.40	Leech Creek	Yes	1	4	
22	0.44	Leech Creek	No	0	0	Scattered stand, not much aspen
23	1.16	Leech Creek	Yes	2	8	
24	0.33	Leech Creek	Yes	1	3	
25	0.36	Leech Creek	No	0	0	Shrubby snow damaged aspen
26	1.53	Leech Creek	Yes	3	12	
27	0.38	Cottonwood Creek Area	Yes	1	3	
28	3.55	Cottonwood Creek Area	No	0	0	Shrubby snow damaged aspen
29	0.61	Cottonwood Creek Area	Yes	1	4	
30	0.64	Cottonwood Creek Area	Yes	1	3	
31	0.96	Cottonwood Creek Area	No	0	0	Shrubby snow damaged aspen
32	2.16	Cottonwood Creek Area	Yes	2	8	
33	0.78	Cottonwood Creek Area	Yes	1	3	
34	2.61	Big Cinder Cone	No	2	8	Difficult access, sensitive ecology

Appendix B. Distance Photos in CRMO
Comparison between 2007 and 2010

2010   2007

CRMO-5

CRMO-7

CRMO-9

CRMO10

No photograph in 2007

CRMO-11

CRMO-12

CRMO-13

CRMO-14

CRMO-16

CRMO-17

CRMO-18

No photograph in 2007

CRMO-20

CRMO-21

CRMO-23

CRMO-24

CRMO-26

CRMO-27

CRMO-29

CRMO-30

CRMO-32

No photograph in 2007

CRMO-33

Appendix C. R code for trend analysis of aspen counts

```
Aspen<-read.table("Aspen.txt", sep="\t", header=TRUE)
dim(Aspen)
names(Aspen)
Aspen$Stand<-as.factor(Aspen$Stand)
Aspen$Transect<-as.factor(Aspen$Transect)
Aspen$Plot<-as.factor(Aspen$Plot)

# Across age groups for raw counts for plots < transects < stands

fit.all.11<-lm(log(TreeCount) ~ -1+ AgeGroup + Stand, data=Aspen)
summary(fit.all.11)

# Stand-level means were calculated in another software
# application and saved in a tab-delimited text file

AspenMean<-read.table("AspenMean.txt", sep="\t", header=TRUE)
AspenMean$Y1<- AspenMean$Year==2007
AspenMean$Y2<- 1-AspenMean$Y1
AspenMean$Stand<-as.factor(AspenMean$Stand)

# Stand-level means

fit9<-lm(log(MeanTreeCount) ~ -1+AgeGroup, data=AspenMean)
summary(fit9)

# Within age groups – stand-level means

# Suckers

fitS3<-lm(log(MeanTreeCount) ~ -1 + Y1 + Stand, data=Aspen.S)
summary(fitS3)

# Regen

fitR7<-lm(log(MeanTreeCount) ~ -1 + Y1, data=Aspen.R)
summary(fitR7)

# Mature

fitM3<-lm(log(MeanTreeCount) ~ -1 + Y1 + Stand, data=Aspen.M)
summary(fitM3)

# Dead

fitD9<-lm(log(MeanTreeCount) ~ -1+ Stand, data=Aspen.D)
summary(fitD9)
```

Apendix D. R code for trend models for conifer counts

Copy and paste these functions into R. Note that the functions will need to be amended to reflect the best model for the outcome. Model selection was conducted using BIC.

```
expit<-function(x)  return(exp(x) / (1 + exp(x)))

ZILN_MLE_ALL_FULL<- function(parms,vars, data){

tmp<-rep(0,5)
names(tmp)<-c("pconst","psiconst", "Y1", "AgeS.zi", "sigma2")
tmp[vars]<-parms

OccData<-ZIData<-c(0,1)
M<-J<-2

Rows<- dim(data)[1]
ones<-rep(1,M)
y1<- OccData
ageS.zi<- ZIData

# Model detection probs:
p<-expit(tmp[1]+tmp[4]*ageS.zi)
# Model occupancy rates
mu<- tmp[2]*ones + tmp[3]*y1
LogLik<-rep(1,M)
ymat<-data$MeanTreeCount

for(i in 1:M){                                          # Site loop
prob.site.i<-rep(1,J)
        for(j in 1:J){                                  # Site loop
index<-(1:Rows)*as.numeric((data$Y1== OccData[i]) & (data$AgeS== ZIData[j]))
index<-index[index!=0]
m<-length(index)
if(m>0)  {
                yvec<-ymat[index]
# Calc Log likelihood
prob.site<- (p[j]*(yvec==0)) + ((1-p[j])* dlnorm(yvec, meanlog = mu[i], sdlog = sqrt(tmp[5])))
prob.site.i[j]<- prod(prob.site)
                }                                       # end if
        }                                               # end j loop
# Calc prob of occurrence for each site
        LogLik[i]<-log(prod(prob.site.i))
  }                                                     # End site loop
sum(-1*LogLik)
}
```

```
ZILN_MLE_ALL_RED<- function(parms,vars, data){

tmp<-rep(0,5)
names(tmp)<-c("pconst","psiconst", "AgeS.zi", "sigma2")
tmp[vars]<-parms

OccData<-ZIData<-c(0,1)
J<-2
M<-1

Rows<- dim(data)[1]
ones<-rep(1,M)
y1<- OccData
ageS.zi<- ZIData

# Model detection probs:
p<-expit(tmp[1]+tmp[4]*ageS.zi)
# Model occupancy rates
mu<- tmp[2]*ones
LogLik<-rep(1,M)
ymat<-data$MeanTreeCount

for(i in 1:M){                                          # Site loop
prob.site.i<-rep(1,J)
        for(j in 1:J){                                 # Site loop
index<-(1:Rows)*as.numeric((data$Y1== OccData[i]) & (data$AgeS== ZIData[j]))
index<-index[index!=0]
m<-length(index)
if(m>0)  {
                    yvec<-ymat[index]
# Calc Log likelihood
prob.site<- (p[j]*(yvec==0)) + ((1-p[j])* dlnorm(yvec, meanlog = mu[i], sdlog = sqrt(tmp[5])))
prob.site.i[j]<- prod(prob.site)
                    }                                  # end if
        }                                              # end j loop
# Calc prob of occurrence for each site
    LogLik[i]<-log(prod(prob.site.i))
  }                                                    # End site loop
  sum(-1*LogLik)
}
```

```
ZILN_MLE_AgeClass_FULL<- function(parms,vars, data){

tmp<-rep(0,4)
names(tmp)<-c("pconst","psiconst", "Y1", "sigma2")
tmp[vars]<-parms

OccData<- c(0,1)
M<- 2

Rows<- dim(data)[1]
ones<-rep(1,M)
y1<- OccData

# Model detection probs:
p<-expit(tmp[1])
# Model occupancy rates
mu<- tmp[2]*ones + tmp[3]*y1
LogLik<-rep(1,M)
ymat<-data$MeanTreeCount
prob.site.i<-rep(1,M)

for(i in 1:M){                                              # Site loop
index<-(1:Rows)*as.numeric(data$Y1== OccData[i])
index<-index[index!=0]
m<-length(index)
if(m>0)  {
                    yvec<-ymat[index]

# Calc Log likelihood
prob.site<- (p*(yvec==0)) + ((1-p)* dlnorm(yvec, meanlog = mu[i], sdlog = sqrt(tmp[4])))
prob.site.i[i]<- prod(prob.site)
                    }                                      # end if
# Calc prob of occurrence for each site
LogLik[i]<-log(prob.site.i[i])
          }                                                # End site loop
sum(-1*LogLik)
}
```

```
ZILN_MLE_AgeClass_RED<- function(parms,vars, data){

tmp<-rep(0,3)
names(tmp)<-c("pconst","psiconst", "sigma2")
tmp[vars]<-parms
Rows<- dim(data)[1]
ones<-rep(1,Rows)

# Model detection probs:
p<-expit(tmp[1])
# Model occupancy rates
mu<- tmp[2]
ymat<-data$MeanTreeCount

# Calc Log likelihood
prob.site<- (p*(ymat==0)) + ((1-p)* dlnorm(ymat, meanlog = mu, sdlog = sqrt(tmp[3])))
LogLik<-log(prod(prob.site))
sum(-1*LogLik)
}


# Format data
# The data set "ConiferMean.txt" was obtained from Eva Strand.
# Stand-level means of tree counts are obtained with the following
# function.

Conifer<-read.table("Conifer.txt", sep="\t", header=TRUE)
Conifer$Stand<-as.factor(Conifer$Stand)
Conifer$Transect<-as.factor(Conifer$Transect)
Conifer$Plot<-as.factor(Conifer$Plot)

ConiferMean2<-tapply(Conifer$TreeCount, list(Conifer$Year, Conifer$Stand, Conifer$AgeGroup), mean)

FormatData<-function(v) {

stands<-sort(unique(Conifer$Stand))
n<-length(stands)
ages<- sort(unique(Conifer$AgeGroup))
m<-length(ages)
yrs<- sort(unique(Conifer$Year))
y<-length(yrs)
index<-0
answer<-data.frame(matrix(0, n*m*y, 4))
for (i in 1:n) {
        for (j in 1:m) {
                for (k in 1:y) {
                        index<- index+1
                        answer[index,]<-c(yrs[k], stands[i], ages[j], v[k,i,j])
                }

        }
}
answer[answer[,3]==1,3]<-"Dead"
answer[answer[,3]==2,3]<-"Mature"
answer[answer[,3]==3,3]<-"Regen"
answer[answer[,3]==4,3]<-"Sucker"
```

```
names(answer)<-c("Year", "Stand", "AgeGroup", "MeanTreeCount")
return(answer)
}

ConiferMean <-FormatData(ConiferMean2)

ConiferMean$Y1<- as.numeric(ConiferMean$Year==2007)
ConiferMean$Y2<- 1-ConiferMean$Y1
ConiferMean$Stand<-as.factor(ConiferMean$Stand)
ConiferMean$AgeS<- as.numeric(ConiferMean$AgeGroup=="Sucker")
ConiferMean$AgeR<- as.numeric(ConiferMean$AgeGroup=="Regen")
ConiferMean$AgeM<- as.numeric(ConiferMean$AgeGroup=="Mature")
ConiferMean$AgeD<- as.numeric(ConiferMean$AgeGroup=="Dead")

ConiferMean.S<- ConiferMean[ConiferMean$AgeGroup=="Sucker",]
ConiferMean.R<- ConiferMean[ConiferMean$AgeGroup=="Regen",]
ConiferMean.M<- ConiferMean[ConiferMean$AgeGroup=="Mature",]
ConiferMean.D<- ConiferMean[ConiferMean$AgeGroup=="Dead",]
```

Test for change between years across all age classes

```
# Get starting values for the log-normal distribution
fit.full.logreg.all<-lm(log(MeanTreeCount+.01) ~ Y1, data=ConiferMean[ConiferMean$MeanTreeCount>0,])
summary(fit.full.logreg.all)
# Get starting values for the zero-inflation distribution
fit.full.ZI<-glm(((MeanTreeCount==0)) ~ AgeS, family=binomial, data= ConiferMean)
summary(fit.full.ZI)

v.all.full= c("pconst","psiconst", "Y1", "sigma2", "AgeS.zi")
mle.all.full<-nlm(ZILN_MLE_ALL_FULL, p= c(fit.full.ZI$coef[1], fit.full.logreg.all$coef,
summary(fit.full.logreg.all)$sigma^2, fit.full.ZI$coef[2]),vars= v.all.full, data=ConiferMean, hessian=TRUE,
iterlim=100000, steptol=0.000000000001)
mle.all.full
```

Conduct trend test using the likelihood ratio test
Obtain a reduced model that excludes the year term in the lognormal model
Compare the full model to the reduced model to determine if the year coefficient is
significantly different than zero:

```
fit.full.logreg.red<-lm(log(MeanTreeCount+.01) ~ 1, data=ConiferMean[ConiferMean$MeanTreeCount>0,])
summary(fit.full.logreg.red)
v.all.red= c("pconst","psiconst", "sigma2", "AgeS.zi")
mle.all.red<-nlm(ZILN_MLE_ALL_FULL, p= c(fit.full.ZI$coef[1], fit.full.logreg.red$coef,
summary(fit.full.logreg.red)$sigma^2, fit.full.ZI$coef[2]),vars= v.all.red, data=ConiferMean, hessian=TRUE,
iterlim=100000, steptol=0.000000000001)
mle.all.red
```

Note that the reduced model may not have a positive-definite Hessian matrix,
but that will not affect the results of the likelihood ratio test. Obtain the
likelihood ratio test statistic:

```
# Likelihood ratio test
chisq.all<- 2*(mle.all.red$minimum - mle.all.full$minimum)
p.value.all<-pchisq(chisq.all, 1, lower.tail=FALSE)
round(c(chisq.all, p.value.all), 4)
1.3784 0.2404
```

```
# Testing at the 0.05 level, the p-value of 0.2404 indicates no significant change in stand-
# level means of conifer counts between the two years.
```

```
# Suckers
```

```
v.S.full= c("pconst","psiconst", "Y1", "sigma2")
fit.S.full.logreg.S<-lm(log(MeanTreeCount+.01) ~ Y1, data=ConiferMean.S[ConiferMean.S$MeanTreeCount>0,])
summary(fit.S.full.logreg.S)
fit.S.full.ZI<-glm(((MeanTreeCount==0)) ~ 1, family=binomial, data= ConiferMean.S)
summary(fit.S.full.ZI)
```

```
mle.S.full<-nlm(ZILN_MLE_AgeClass_FULL, p= c(fit.S.full.ZI$coef, fit.S.full.logreg.S$coef,
summary(fit.S.full.logreg.S)$sigma^2),vars= v.S.full, data=ConiferMean.S,  hessian=TRUE, iterlim=100000,
steptol=0.000000000001)
mle.S.full
```

```
# reduced model
fit.S.full.logreg.red<-lm(log(MeanTreeCount+.01) ~ 1, data=ConiferMean.S[ConiferMean.S$MeanTreeCount>0,])
summary(fit.S.full.logreg.red)
v.S.red= c("pconst","psiconst", "sigma2")
mle.S.red<-nlm(ZILN_MLE_AgeClass_RED, p= c(fit.S.full.ZI$coef, fit.S.full.logreg.red$coef,
summary(fit.S.full.logreg.red)$sigma^2),vars= v.S.red, data=ConiferMean.S,  hessian=TRUE, iterlim=100000,
steptol=0.000000000001)
mle.S.red
```

```
# Likelihood ratio test
chisq.S<- 2*(mle.S.red$minimum - mle.S.full$minimum)
p.value.S<-pchisq(chisq.S, 1, lower.tail=FALSE)
round(c(chisq.S, p.value.S), 4)
0.5027 0.4783
```

```
# Testing at the 0.05 level, the p-value of 0.4783 indicates no significant change in stand-
# level means of conifer counts between the two years.
```

Regeneration

```
v.R.full= c("pconst","psiconst", "Y1", "sigma2")
fit.R.full.logreg.R<-lm(log(MeanTreeCount+.01) ~ Y1,
data=ConiferMean.R[ConiferMean.R$MeanTreeCount>0,])
summary(fit.R.full.logreg.R)
fit.R.full.ZI<-glm(((MeanTreeCount==0)) ~ 1, family=binomial, data= ConiferMean.R)
summary(fit.R.full.ZI)

mle.R.full<-nlm(ZILN_MLE_AgeClass_FULL, p= c(fit.R.full.ZI$coef, fit.R.full.logreg.R$coef,
summary(fit.R.full.logreg.R)$sigma^2),vars= v.R.full, data=ConiferMean.R, hessian=TRUE, iterlim=100000,
steptol=0.000000000001)
mle.R.full

# reduced model
fit.R.full.logreg.red<-lm(log(MeanTreeCount+.01) ~ 1, data=ConiferMean.R[ConiferMean.R$MeanTreeCount>0,])
summary(fit.R.full.logreg.red)
v.R.red= c("pconst","psiconst", "sigma2")
mle.R.red<-nlm(ZILN_MLE_AgeClass_RED, p= c(fit.R.full.ZI$coef, fit.R.full.logreg.red$coef,
summary(fit.R.full.logreg.red)$sigma^2),vars= v.R.red, data=ConiferMean.R, hessian=TRUE, iterlim=100000,
steptol=0.000000000001)
mle.R.red

# Likelihood ratio test
chisq.R<- 2*(mle.R.red$minimum - mle.R.full$minimum)
p.value.R<-pchisq(chisq.R, 1, lower.tail=FALSE)
round(c(chisq.R, p.value.R), 4)
0.0509 0.8216
```

Testing at the 0.05 level, the p-value of 0.8216 indicates no significant change in stand-
level means of conifer counts between the two years.

Mature

```
v.M.full= c("pconst","psiconst", "Y1", "sigma2")
fit.M.full.logreg.M<-lm(log(MeanTreeCount+.01) ~ Y1,
data=ConiferMean.M[ConiferMean.M$MeanTreeCount>0,])
summary(fit.M.full.logreg.M)
fit.M.full.ZI<-glm(((MeanTreeCount==0)) ~ 1, family=binomial, data= ConiferMean.M)
summary(fit.M.full.ZI)

mle.M.full<-nlm(ZILN_MLE_AgeClass_FULL, p= c(fit.M.full.ZI$coef, fit.M.full.logreg.M$coef,
summary(fit.M.full.logreg.M)$sigma^2),vars= v.M.full, data=ConiferMean.M, hessian=TRUE, iterlim=100000,
steptol=0.000000000001)
mle.M.full

# reduced model
fit.M.full.logreg.red<-lm(log(MeanTreeCount+.01) ~ 1,
data=ConiferMean.M[ConiferMean.M$MeanTreeCount>0,])
summary(fit.M.full.logreg.red)
v.M.red= c("pconst","psiconst", "sigma2")
mle.M.red<-nlm(ZILN_MLE_AgeClass_RED, p= c(fit.M.full.ZI$coef, fit.M.full.logreg.red$coef,
summary(fit.M.full.logreg.red)$sigma^2),vars= v.M.red, data=ConiferMean.M, hessian=TRUE, iterlim=100000,
steptol=0.000000000001)
mle.M.red

# Likelihood ratio test
chisq.M<- 2*(mle.M.red$minimum - mle.M.full$minimum)
p.value.M<-pchisq(chisq.M, 1, lower.tail=FALSE)
round(c(chisq.M, p.value.M), 4)
8.6610 0.0033

# Testing at the 0.05 level, the p-value of 0.0033 indicates a significant change in stand-
# level means of conifer counts between the two years.
```

Dead

```
v.D.full= c("pconst","psiconst", "Y1", "sigma2")
fit.D.full.logreg.D<-lm(log(MeanTreeCount+.01) ~ Y1,
data=ConiferMean.D[ConiferMean.D$MeanTreeCount>0,])
summary(fit.D.full.logreg.D)
fit.D.full.ZI<-glm(((MeanTreeCount==0)) ~ 1, family=binomial, data= ConiferMean.D)
summary(fit.D.full.ZI)

mle.D.full<-nlm(ZILN_MLE_AgeClass_FULL, p= c(fit.D.full.ZI$coef, fit.D.full.logreg.D$coef[1],0,
summary(fit.D.full.logreg.D)$sigma^2),vars= v.D.full, data=ConiferMean.D, hessian=TRUE, iterlim=100000,
steptol=0.000000000001)
mle.D.full

# reduced model
fit.D.full.logreg.red<-lm(log(MeanTreeCount+.01) ~ 1,
data=ConiferMean.D[ConiferMean.D$MeanTreeCount>0,])
summary(fit.D.full.logreg.red)
v.D.red= c("pconst","psiconst", "sigma2")
mle.D.red<-nlm(ZILN_MLE_AgeClass_RED, p= c(fit.D.full.ZI$coef, fit.D.full.logreg.red$coef,
summary(fit.D.full.logreg.red)$sigma^2),vars= v.D.red, data=ConiferMean.D, hessian=TRUE, iterlim=100000,
steptol=0.000000000001)
mle.D.red

# Likelihood ratio test
chisq.D<- 2*(mle.D.red$minimum - mle.D.full$minimum)
p.value.D<-pchisq(chisq.D, 1, lower.tail=FALSE)
round(c(chisq.D, p.value.D), 4)


# Note that the hessian matrix is singular in the full fit by using:
solve(mle.D.full$hessian)


# Because there are no non-zero observations of dead conifers in 2010, the full model
# including the year term cannot be fit. Therefore, no test for trend may be obtained for
# these data.
```

NPS 963/107782, June 2011

www.ingramcontent.com/pod-product-compliance
Lightning Source LLC
Chambersburg PA
CBHW080909290526
45795CB00007BA/2470